Sunrise Hearts ©2018 by Petar Kostadinov

Sunrise Hearts

By

Petar Kostadinov

Sunrise Hearts ©2018 by Petar Kostadinov

Copyright Page

Published by www.pajkpublishing.com
Printed through wwwcreatespace.com

FIRST EDITION

©2018 by Petar Kostadinov
All rights reserved. No part of this book can be Reproduced in any form without the written consent from the publisher and the author; including photocopy, recording, or any storage information and retrieval system, without the written permission of the copyright owner.

The book of this work is fiction. Any resemblance to places, people, is purely coincidental.

ISBN-13: 978-4568901962
ISBN-10: 4568901960

Sunrise Hearts ©2018 by Petar Kostadinov

Contents Book Sunrise Hearts ♥

Waking Up in the middle 5
Squeeze Me   6
You Are Here In My Heart 7
My Love Forever Will Stand For You 8
Your Smile 9
Sunrise Hearts 10
I Love To 11
Love You Like Crazy 12
And I Cherish You For Life 13
You Are my Ecstasy 14
As The Wind Blows Slowly 15
Simple Lives 16
Unbroken Wings 17
Hold Me In The morning 18
What I am looking for 19
The Car He Packed 20
Tough 21
I want To Sing With You 22
Like A Broken Sea 23
I Still Love You 24
Like A River 25
Magic 26
Loving Every Minute 27
Think About You 28
Silvery Lights 29
So Shine On 30
My Heart 31
Deep Blue Sea 32
Putting On A Show 33
Hideaway 34
I've Fallen For You 35
And Yet Again 36
Eleven Reasons Why 37
Walk Me Jesus 38
Stolen Hearts 39
Rewind Us 40
I Don't have to Sing every Song 41
One and only 42

You Are my world 43
Of Million Heartbeats 44
Not A true light 45
Never Mind The Sun 46
This Is What We Are 47
Tell it like it is   48
Baby It's You   49
And Your Scent Still Lingers 50
Two Oceans 51
You are my Puzzle Of Love 52
Not So Sure Anymore 53
It's the magical ordinary life 54
My Supernova 55
Regrets 56
Steady 57
You Are My Northern Lights 58
Two Other People 59
This I Can Do For You 60
I Favorite You In My soul 61
In My Soul 62
You Are My Easy Light 63
Write You A Song 64
Crystal Bowl 65
Temptation 66
Sunshine and Glamour 67
Baby Save Me 68
Give Me Five Million Reasons 69
Epitome 70

Waking up in the middle

(Chorus)
Waking up in the middle
Of the morning rise
Seeing your smile
In my dreams and they are wild
Baby you are my sunshine through
The rain on those cloudy days

And you are welcome in my heart
Always in my soul and even as I leave
To go and be with the Lord one day
You will be loved by me

And picture can say a thousand words
It can bring us back in one beating day
Sunrise in the morning beautiful day

(Chorus)

I love you greatly
I love you madly
I love you deeply
From my heart

Seven days a week
Twelve months of the year
Thinking about you
Is all I do Forever

(Chorus)

Squeeze me

(Chorus)
Squeeze me
Love me Need me
When the day rises
When the night sleeps

You are my golden grace
Faithful love
Beautiful in all you are
To me you are my everything

My heart beating for you
Each time I see you
My soul trembles
You make me fly
Through the skies

(Chorus)

You are my sunshine
My superhero
Baby you are my days
And nights my graceful lights

Let's just relax
Be us tonight
Let's just dance
Through this magical
Mystery life

(Chorus)

You Are here in my heart

I have not heard from you
In three whole weeks
Baby I am thinking about you
Your smile driving crazy wild

Hope you are doing alright
Hope you are chasing your heart
Hope you are chasing your dreams
Tonight today tomorrow

(Chorus)
This is how my heart goes
Breaking every emotion motion
Single day life on the Thankful grace
I am breathing alright knowing
You are here in my heart

So please let me know
If you are alright
I am here patiently waiting
Waiting on your love
Every single day
And I am lost in this timeline

(Chorus)
(Repeat Chorus 2 more times
Plus the last line of the chorus)

My love forever will stand for you

I will never lose faith in us baby
I will never lose faith in you
You guide me you heal me
You are my beautiful angel

Every day every step of the way
You are here with me even when
I am far away in this distance
Across oceans of love oceans of life

(Chorus)
And everything that stands
In-between us know they will lose
We always have each other
Even when the moon shines in through
My love forever will stand for you

So reach for me reach for my heart
Call my name and I'll be right there
Will fly like Superman to save your day
This I promise you out of my heart

(Chorus)
And everything that stands
In-between us know they will lose
We always have each other
Even when the moon shines in through
My love forever will stand for you

Your smile

Like a great day
On a stormy sea
You came my way
And rescued me

You looked at me
Said hello to me
That beautiful song
That you sang to me

(Chorus)
Darling your smile
Just lifts my heart higher
Your love just puts my soul
At ease and mind

I live to be with you
If you call me I will be there
Right away no need to worry
Baby you are my only friend
My forever destiny

Looking at you Looking at me
Beautiful dream In our story
Made possible from one simple day
When you said hello to my heart

(Chorus)
Darling your smile
Just lifts my heart higher
Your love just puts my soul
At ease and mind

Sunrise Hearts
___

Beauty in heart
Song that lights
Promise of destiny
Designing history
Over with time
Our souls forever lifted up

I love to
———————-

This song I sing for you
For the rest of my life
Loving you for the rest of your life

Baby you are my beautiful
That hold on moment
I give in each time
You hold me right

(Chorus)
Easy and fun
Slow as we glow
Through the nighttime
Every time every ride
I love to

No better way
But always true
You can be
I can be
We can be us
Together forever

Hopeful stronger
They can try to tear us
They can try to break us
We will always stick like glue
Together till the end of our time

(Chorus)

Love you like crazy
———————————-

(Chorus)
Love you like crazy
Need you Like breezy morning
Lights shining
you are my only one
Touch of the chorus line
Keeps me singing on and on

Even If the season changes
You are my golden star
Every time no matter what
It is you my heart cannot
Love without live without

Unbroken light
Sincerely my mind
Brighter as song
Singing me sweet times

(Chorus)

Don't care about that
Crazy world out there
All I see is your sweet smile
Shining back at me

This forever
This amazing
This promise
This sea time
Best of life
My lucky star

(Chorus)

And I Cherish you for life

In a blink of an eye
In a moments Divine
In a heartbeat of light
You gave me your heart

I love you back
From each step of my mind
I give you all of me to you
Every breath given day I take

(Chorus)

No road that crumbles
Can stop us from us
No worries or thunder
Can break our vows
Our world are our stories
Combined into one sea

You hold me true
You hold me right
You hold me graceful
Every single day By your side
Through morning and night

(Chorus)
Baby you are my gift
That Deals me right
From Dear Lords graceful Heart
when he painted you for me
And I cherish you for life

  (Repeat Chorus)
  (Repeat last line from the chorus)

You Are my ecstasy
———————————-

(Chorus)
You are my ecstasy
My true Divine
My beautiful song
Singing me right

Tender through the night
Easy ride through the daylight
Flying me through those sky highs
Feeling great with you all the time

This story we write together
Drifting away into that sunshine
Incredible sense of days
Flowing through Those
majestic seas of grace

(Chorus)

Thanks to you
I am alive and free
Thanks to you
I am beautiful and sunshine warm
Every day of my life
Every breath I subside

When you call me up
I rush over to heal your heart
When you call my name
I stop by and reach for your hand
Holding on to you giving my mind
To you my love

(Chorus)

Sunrise Hearts ©2018 by Petar Kostadinov

As the wind blows Slowly
———————————-

Every dream
Every time
Every rhyme
Gracefully sweeter

This weather keeps us
Lightning thunder
Our hearts just proves
to be lighter

(Chorus)
as the wind blows slowly
Tenderly you are my beautiful sea
Flowing through my heart
And Everything about you
Makes me feel safer

And it takes million dreams
It takes million stars
To reach out to you
To be with you baby

Everything about you
That keeps my soul alive
Everything about you
That makes my mind alive
Flowing by and by

(Chorus)

You are my rock star
Amazing thunder
That my heart hungers

Better times
Sunshine heaven
Embraced by your heart
Makes me feel alive

(Chorus)(Repeat 1st line from the chorus)

Simple lives
————————-

Living my life In perfect storm
Chasing this dream Like I always been

And you come along Rescue me
Taking my hand Staring at my eyes
Deeply in love

(Chorus)
Looking at your heart
Pouring me good mornings
With your every smile
Living life together
We have this simple life Simple lives

I am yours forever
I am yours till my golden heart
Stops turning clockwise
Running to you
Even when I am a ghost
Saving you Protecting you
From those bad storms reaching to you

(Chorus)

I give you my love I give you my heart
I give you my number Call me when you are
Feeling down Reach me by the Message box
Text me into the night I will wake up listening
Holding on to your love You are delicate rose
Flying through the winds Smiling to the sea

(Chorus)

Sunrise Hearts ©2018 by Petar Kostadinov

Unbroken wings
―――――――

As I am
As we are
This is our first line
Riding through
This place
We call love

Everything that shines
Everything that applies
God gave me you
To be loved to cherish you
To hold you love you
Respect you

(Chorus)
You gave me sweet dreams
You brought me sweet songs
To sing along and you gave me
Unbroken wings to fly next to you

Everything that times
Everything that rhymes
Beauty in within

You are my possibilities
You are my golden sea
Passing through those
Fields of dreams

(Chorus)

Hold me in the morning
———————————-

The weather looks great today
It looks like it will sprinkle a little
There is that sound of heaven flowing
Right through my mind

I am longing for you
Each moment
Just as the sunshine
Warms us up
You are my golden angel
Saving me saving my heart

(Chorus)
So be there for me
Just like this
Hold me in the morning
Before the sunrise comes through

This is where we belong
Together in our own Good storm
Tangled with love
Underneath this lace bed sheets

I give you my soul
I give you my mind
I give you my heart
All that is great in me
I give you my breath
I take the air with

(Chorus)
(Repeat Chorus 2 Times
Plus the 3rd line of the chorus)

What I am looking for
———————-

If I could ring a thousand bells
If I could time a thousand stars
If I could rhyme thousand words
All would sound just for you

Just as your sweet
Just as your beautiful
Like a delicate flower
Smiling in the summer wind

(Chorus)
You are my golden heart
Bringing me hope
Through my mind
Love of endless laughs
Singing songs of endless grace
And what I am looking for
Is your smile next to my beating heart

I would forever be yours
I would forever live to love you
Sweeter to tenderly

And ask me and I will
Bring you back to life
Dreams to help you built upon
Those heavenly skies

(Chorus)

The Car He packed
———————————

He can see the endless hope
One dream that lists his life
Every page perfectly written
As it breaks his heart
The way she had him
In the palm of her hands

They loved They sang together
Everything seemed
Like they were never
going to Break up

(Chorus)
The car he packed
Day by day
Ready to leave Any day
Knowing he would be back

As he looked at his kids eyes
Trying not to go and say goodbye
The fights the screams from her
Every single day as he tried to heal his
Wounds she thundered inside and out on him

Long days
History made
Make it all sense
Senseless game

(Chorus)

Sunrise Hearts ©2018 by Petar Kostadinov

Tough
————

Gotta be stronger
Gotta be braver
Every road takes us down
Beats us rough

There is one wind
There is one song
One dream and you know
Which I am speaking about

(Chorus)
I would be tough
No matter what bring me down
Just dancing all the way
Even if they push me rough

I need you mostly
I need you closely
Baby you are my rock
The roughest strive
This soul of my own needs
I am tough because of your love
To protect you forever

Destiny reality
Flowing by the sunshine sea
Walking with you on that sand
Paradise

(Chorus)

I want to sing with you
————————-

(Chorus)
I want to sing with you
I want to swing with you
I want to dance with you
All night long
All day long baby I do

Lets make good memories
Lets just feel free
This thunder storm
Coming from our hearts
Pounding so hard

Missing you so much
Missing to kiss your sweet lips
Want a drown in your love
Baby you are my hero
Saving my life
Making it all better

(Chorus)
(Repeat Chorus)
(Repeat first line of the chorus)

Like a broken sea

How can you say you want me
When you don't even know me
Feels like a sunny day
Feels like a dream today

Everything is alright
When you are with me
In this paradise
Dancing in the moonlight

(Chorus)
I am just getting back to me
Like a broken sea
Blistered and blue
Inside my soul

It takes millions stars
To get me back
Through this Christmas breaks
Torn in two fields

And I still want you
Still need you
Still ache about you
Like rainy night
Just holding on

(Chorus)

I Still Love You
_____

(Chorus)
I still love you
Everything about you
Every smile you turn me on
You heal my heart

I am your biggest fan
Baby you are my sunshine days
Can't live without you my honey bee
You make me feel happy

I need you I love you
Every road We are together
Every single time
Hope that shines through me

(Chorus)

You give me hope
You give me days ahead
Out those storms
Brighter sunshine

Healing my soul
Healing my heart
Healing this broken smile
Turning it upside down

(Chorus)

Like A River

I drove all night
Thinking about us
I drove with my heart
Thanks to you
I just feel uneasy tonight

You told me you cared
You told me you will be forever
You told me you will be here
One light and it just turned off
Broke off into the darkness

(Chorus)
Like a river
One strong to shine
The other kind of dreary
It takes better you
To come back to better us

I am heavy inside
I am broken with tears
Every ounce of my body
Just crumbles into smaller ashes

And I drift away waiting for hope
Singing tunes we used to sing together
In my car when I am alone
When I tune out that world
Just us in my heart

(Chorus)
Like a river
One strong to shine
The other kind of dreary
It takes better you
To come back to better us

(Chorus)
(Repeat Chorus)

Magic

I am breathing Living life
You know I am just Alright
Feeling beautiful inside

Right about now
Thinking about you
Right about now
I am counting stars
In our universe

(Chorus)
Ever since you came
into my life
Baby you give me
Magic the number one
Road where I need to be
Right now

I am yours forever
Every inch of my soul
Every inch of my body
You can have me Faithfully

I run to you
Every time you call me up
I long for you every time
You are far from me

(Chorus)

Loving Every Minute

The moment
You came into my life
My heart kept on
Drumming up

Sound up
Around this world
That magical touch
Those heavenly eyes
You are to me
One beautiful dream

(Chorus)
I will be yours forever
I will be there in your arms
Loving every minute
Nothing will ever change that

You are my golden angel
Protecting me baby
You are my golden heart
Tenderly healing me

Every joy
Everything about you
Everything that stands out
Dancing with you
through the nighttime

(Chorus)
(Repeat Chorus)

Think about you

Given my heart
To a breaking road
Over those skies
Highway ninety nine

I look at those stars
Counting them all
Looking for you
Be with you tonight

(Chorus)
All I ever need
Is your sweet lips
Smiling right back to me
Feeling better forever
Think about you

Night and day
You are part of my life
You are heating my soul
You fill my heart with sunshine

I love you
You hold the key
To my dreams
To my heart

(Chorus)
(Repeat Chorus)

Silvery lights
———————-

What am I singing for?
Why do I have to be this way?
Easy like a flight feathered bird
Music sounds of you again

I give into you
Every best of me to you
You made me feel
As though I was not living

Shine on me
God speak to me
Lead me back to you
Into existence

(Chorus)
I want to have
Golden wings
Upon this
Silvery lights

What makes me happy
Is being free from this sea
It feels uneasy as I am floating
Through this mystery

I watched it all
Have been here to love
and Love I leave
The way you told me to bear

(Chorus)

So Shine on
————————

God gave you peace of mind
To look at daylight
Road to uncover life
With journeys you bring alive

Every river
Gives you home
Every star
Gives you sunshine warmth
Don't give up on you

(Chorus)
Twenty days
And twenty nights
Being you is greatest you
So shine on

Walk on by those seas
Touch those magical stones
Become a brand new soul
Living in you is your beautiful

Dream of paradise
String on a guitar
Playing softer sides
Must be so nice
To hear yourself dance

(Chorus)

My Heart
———-

You come to mind
Every walk I walk
Every small break I take
Every time I see those
Perfumes out in that storefront
Signs

You take my breath away
Every single time
You look at me
With your beautiful smile
Heaven must have smiled
Down at me when he send me you

(Chorus)
This feeling is magical
My Heart keeps on
Singing lights
I am breathing fine

You keep me laughing
You keep me busy
You keep me living
Loving you so easy

Don't forget you are my
Goldenrod heaven of sunshine
Superwoman

(Chorus)

Deep Blue Sea
―――――――-

All I ever need
All I ever want
To reach out to your
Sweet loving heart

I live on with those stars
Brighter as daylight
Feeding my soul
Just making me breathe
Alright

(Chorus)
So come on hold me right
Like deep blue sea
Sunshine flowing
Looking at me
Looking at you
Just feels alright

You are my beautiful escape
Somebody that understands
Peaceful place where my heart
Can lean on

I take you by my heart
Loving you with unbroken wings
You are my destiny
My best friend for life

(Chorus)

Putting On A Show

Wrote down every word
You ever told me
Went over every space
You led me to believe

You fed my mind
With obstacles
Draining my soul
Tornado storms
Heating my heart

(Chorus)
Everything you were
I thought you are not
Songs you put on that radio
putting on a show

So more of us
I asked you to dance
You lied to my face
Made me believe
I was your only one

Morning comes
I try to wake up
Everything of you
Looks like I am going to
Just put in a box
Close it up and lock it up
For the rest of my life

(Chorus)

Hideaway
———————

Broken and tormented
Torn and unsubtle
Getting by with nothing
More then my soul

Where I go?
Where I am
Something changes
By the way you are with me

(Chorus)
You and me
Rocking by that sea
Feeling just fine
Our own hideaway

This couldn't be any better
Sunshine to sunset
Evermore stories of our lives

Beautifully written down
In those pages in that book
We keep on weaving together

(Chorus)

You are my open road
One sweet day
Sweet dreams
Sweet songs
Playing in my head

(Chorus)

I've fallen for you
―――――――――――――-

(Chorus)
I've fallen for you
Like a leaf on a sunny wind
You hold me right
Treat me kindly
Baby your love is just
Super-funny

As we hold each other tight
As we dance into the moonlight
So right so true so tenderly
Every wing you take me flying

I guide my soul
To be with you strongly
This heart only knows one lovely
And that lovely is you my beautiful

(Chorus)

You fill my soul
With everlasting life
Cherishing my mind
I love you always

Without words
You call on me
Those sweet eyes
Smiling back to me
Softly gently

(Chorus)

And Yet Again
―――――――

In twenty four hours
I would try to wake up
Time has given me
after my dream

I saw us there
Making up
Making plans
Just smiling

(Chorus)
And yet again
I would wake up alone
Standing there crying inside
Fighting against all odds
With my heart not to let you go

But you are gone
And there is nothing
No nothing I could ever do
Even if I tried to bring you back
Since you left me stranded here

I love to love you again
Hold you near
To sing you sweet words
I wrote you each night

(Chorus)

Eleven reasons why
_____

And why am I still here
Just wondering
Waiting on you to call me
All this time i know

Every time you are gone
Every time you say
You have to work
I think you are telling me Lies

(Chorus)
How much longer
Does my heart have to beat
For you till I wait
Eleven reasons why

Time has changed
My soul into the universe
Feels like I have gone through
Those skies wishing I could
Ride that boat again

Don't feel like i use to feel
Don't get to where I been
Flown out to work my life out
Woke up in a new body today

(Chorus)

Walk me Jesus
—————————-

Take my hand
Take my time
Keep me breathing
Help me get by and by

(Chorus)
I am your shepherd
So distant yet so close by
Place me in that warmer sun
Walk me Jesus right next to you

This place
This longer road
This app
This water world
Keeps me at bay

As I am living to stay
You are my golden trod
True and loved

(Chorus)

I am blessed
Greatly give thanks
To you that you lead me
Through this passages
Of paradise

(Chorus)

Stolen Hearts

I did not know
What to do
But stand there
And listen to you
Then we parted
Like there was nothing

I just couldn't breathe
I stopped living
Every time your perfume
Flew to my soul

(Chorus)
Stolen hearts
At the end of the night
I lost that feeling One emotion
The moment You got up
and walked Out of my life

Out of my mind
Out of my head
Out of my soul
Trying so hard
To forget you

It isn't easy
It isn't the same
Here without you
I know we left that be
But please come back home
Right where you and I belong

(Chorus)

Rewind Us
———

Like a song
VHS tape
Just press one button
And bring back time
Like it use to be

One dream
One memory
One best of everything
Just give it all a chance

(Chorus)
Baby just
Rewind us
Relax to where we were
One of this days
Harmonize us

I would give my best
To you again
I would give my soul
To you as everlasting love
Peace of my heart

I need you
I love you
I dream of you
When you are
Not around me

(Chorus)

I don't have to sing every song

(Chorus)
I don't have to sing every song
Or dive every ocean
All I ever need is you
Here in my arms
Holding me so right

I am like a Boat
In a sea running on Empty air
'Cause without you
I am just an empty shelf
Without the best of you here

Baby you are my beautiful dream
You are my every channel on that
Tv on and when I click on each
Button you just appear

(Chorus)

all I ever need
Is your sweet surrender
Your sweet lips kissing mine
Before and after daylight

You are an angel
Send from the heavenly skies
To protect my heart
You are my glue to my soul
You are my golden key healing me

(Chorus)

One and only
—————-

My heart wants you
My soul leads to you
You make me happy
You leave me breathless

I walked through
Those skies Of blue rain
You make them Warmer
You are sweet and tender

(Chorus)
I could not know
Much of this song
All I ever know Is you are
My one and only true love

Things inside my heart
Beating to bear your love
I go on missing you
Loving you

Every smell of your perfume
Just hits me right in my head
You are my great escape
Beautiful rain

(Chorus)

You Are My World
————————-

I am drowning in deep water
And you come and pull me out
Rescue me with every single
Breath you have

Very moment
One emotion
Your love
Just puts me at ease

(Chorus)

I feel better when you are
Around me
I feel your heartbeat
Close to my chest
Every time you are near me

You are my favorite song
You are my best of the news
I want to hear all day long
Baby you are my beautiful

(Chorus)
You are my world
You are my rock
You are my golden skies
Angel send from above

Of million heartbeats
————————-

The air I breathe
The skin deep my heart heals
You fill my soul with your beautiful
Laughter unimaginable

You take my hand
As web and we dance
Through those seas
Heavenly skies

(Chorus)
You are my destiny
My purity my dream
Of million heartbeats
Incredible place
Where my mind can lean on

Thanks to you
I am here Breathing
Always and forever
You keep amazing me

You keep sending me love
Through my soul
When you reach out in me
To my mind

(Chorus)

Not A true Light
———————

Just the same
Walking out of that rainstorm
Dealt with promise heart
One emotional drop

And asking for friendships
Thanks of sharing those
Pieces of them being there for her
Always

(Chorus)
Not a true light
One given fact
She returns back to his arms
More games more troubles

Those seven nights
Crusting Crying
Over the moonlight
Morning rises

Given for what is worth
She cannot give up
On what his lies pull her in

(Chorus)

Never Mind The sun
_____

Right now for the rest of our lives
Your lips on my lips
Gently through those seas
Making good memories

I feel like flying
When I am in your arms
You give me hope
Beautiful thunder inside
My heart

(Chorus)
Never mind the sun
Never mind the rain
All I ever want is see you
Be with you

My body just shakes
My body just rattles
Always with you
Love your smile
The golden star
Shining me

(Chorus)
Never mind the sun
Never mind the rain
All I ever want is see you
Be with you

(repeat chorus 2-3 times
And the first line of the chorus)

This Is What We Are

The Moment is one ride
The life is one story one song
we are a gift of light
without end just one perfect day

Tell it like it is
—————

Come to me
Let those skylines
Hear you breathing
You have my heart
Thundering

Eyes on you
Eyes on me
So much sweeter
Incredible surrender

(Chorus)
I walk on with you
Talk to me
Tell it like it is
Line by line
Word by word

You give me songs
Just as the wind flies
You are my beautiful
My heartbeat

Don't ever let us go
Unbreakable
Let's just be us tonight
Over every day

(Chorus)

Baby It's You

(Chorus)
Baby it's you
It's you that I want
It's you that I love
It's you that my heart
Stumbles when I speak

You are one of my favorite
Kinds of songs I play on that
Radio station over and over again

You give me sweet and tender love
True love that feels alright
I am breathing fine when you are
With me every time

(Chorus)

You are my beautiful world
Shining me sweeter
In this paradise
In this walk of life

If you want me you got me
I am forever yours
From this moment on
Till my heart stops
Breathing fine music on

(Chorus)

And your scent still lingers
_____

Here it goes again
I have nothing to lose
But my heart again

I miss you every day
I miss you while I am driving
When I am working

(Chorus)
And your scent still lingers
Upon my brain
Every now and then

You come through my heart
Looking for us better then we
Ever were yesterday
About tomorrow

Like raindrops
Falling on my skin
Looking for fresh start
Cleansing our hearts
To love again

(Chorus)

And I am looking at my phone
Checking through my emails
Hoping you will write again
Something beautiful

Something tender
Hoping wishing you were
Here again

(Chorus)

Two oceans
_____

We are one world apart
I just cannot but wonder
Baby you are my sunshine
My beautiful

Living here
One precious day after day another
So lonely without your smile
Look at us how far we have come so far

(Chorus)
You are my golden angel
Saving my life
With every day
And we are two oceans apart
But still in love

No matter what comes
Between us we cross over
Pass on through
We are stronger then those
Windy days

You and I just in each others
Arms just holding each other
Under those covers
Pages unbroken Pages unspoken

(Chorus)

You Are my puzzle of love

Baby you are right there
When I fall to pick me up
You are right there to
Lift me up in one moment

(Chorus)
You are my puzzle of love
You are my dream that never
Stops me from dreaming beautiful

You take my breath away
Every smile you drift my way
Every drop of raindrop
You heal my heart

Within this soul
Lies a better hope
You are my only friend
that gives me tenderness

(Chorus)

You are as beautiful
As those roses Springing out
In spring time

Treasure of beauty Filling my mind
with Beautiful stories
And I miss you every day
Love you with my heart

(Chorus)

Not so sure anymore
_____

This is where I am now
There is you and I
Just distance about yesterday
Here in the darkness of the night

Flowing by the sunshine
You give me signs of love
Loving you with all my heart
Leaving breathless here inside

(Chorus)
I Can't seem but to wonder
If this thing is alright
Don't understand it
When you are not calling in
Not so sure anymore

Best of you is best of me
You gave me preaching lights
To sing with this glowing starlight
Every single night time

And I am just barely surviving
Here without you without your
Beautiful smile the one you gave me
Every day when we said good night
Right at your doorstep

(Chorus)

It's the magical ordinary life

(Chorus)
It's the magical ordinary life
One dream that falls through
Those skylines

Live it up and love you stronger
You are my beautiful angel
My graceful surrender

I am yours if you want me
Nothing will ever change me
You give me peace in my soul
Tonight I love you Slowly Amazing

(Chorus)

And I am blessed to have you
In my life because I believe in you
I believe in us and I breathe alright

You give me that love
That I always looked for
All my life searching for you
Everywhere I went

(Chorus)
(And first line of the chorus repeat
Repeat Chorus 2-3 Times)

My Supernova
───────────

Feeling that roaming heat
Those heavenly words
You drown me with
This is our destiny

I walk my life
To be with you so right
To promise you forever
You are my Gods gift
Sunshine through the rain

(Chorus)
My endless hope
My superhero
My supernova
Riding out with me

And here with you
Is very nice dream
To love you forever
Is to need you
Is to hold you

You are my beautiful treasure
Unspoken song my guiding light
Better half my good dreams
That my heart wants to hold near
You drive my mind celestial clear

(Chorus)

Regrets
————-

What is in my life
You are my beautiful ride
You are my ocean of hope
You are my sweet dreams
My beautiful melody

I live to love you every day
I live to hold you easily
You are taking my breath away
You are my one I run to
Love that surrounds me

(Chorus)
And have no regrets
Have no back time
You know you are my song
I always dance too

I am the best of you
The one you hold true
The reasons you love me
The best thing that
ever happened to me

I breathe good air
I swim that sea
To reach out to you
To your sweet touch

(Chorus)

Steady

Like a Boat in a sea
Driving miles to reach It's stories
highlights of its time Days in history

I am in love with you
You are my golden rod
Trodding so much in my heart
My mind keeps on racing for you

(Chorus)
And I am
Just in this steady fame
Heaven and hope
That is what you are to me
My one and only true love

In scope of things
As this world spins
365 days of the yahoo years
Destiny has in it for us
Something we just cannot
Escape that sunshine

So bring me to you
To love you more
To need you through
Eternal bliss
Te amo mi amor
I Love You

(Chorus)

You Are My Northern lights

Let me kiss you one more time
Last goodbye song
Taking me back
Where my heart goes

Nothing but that sound
Over head in heaven
This I know how well
It's written

(Chorus)
In this aching hour
In this small town
I keep on singing
Your name aloud
You are my Northern lights

Becoming that road
Walking those skies
Shifting around
While I drift in my sleep tonight

Taking my guitar
Writing you sweet sweet
Sounds the ones about us
The way you make feel
make me smile bringing me alive

(Chorus)

Sunrise Hearts ©2018 by Petar Kostadinov

Two other people
_____

This I know
When my heart
Hears your call
Just that rain
Come falling down my skin

With you I am
More then yesterday
Beautiful song shining
Creation of summertime

(Chorus)
And two other people
Holding on forever
Down on that avenue
Of love just like us
Baby that's us

There is not a thing
That I don't love about you
You are my true grace
Leading me on

That rainbow
Peaceful and serene
You are that butterfly
Flying over me near me
Healing me
Protecting me

(Chorus)

Sunrise Hearts ©2018 by Petar Kostadinov

This I can do for you

You use to be there
When my heart needed you most
You use to care when you call my
Name by sound

Sweet as the ocean
Promise you forever
Drifting out into that universe
Our love was unspoken prayer

Baby you are my rock
By the grace of God
You are my beautiful Angel
Singing me sweet lullabies
Morning through nighttime

(Chorus)
And I can spell my song for you
Sing you just as my soul bleeds
Only for you open the door
Hold you up when you are down
I can this I can do for you

Give you all of my attention
Come to you fly to you
From work I will leave and
Be next to you

Bring you coffee
Make you dinner
Make you breakfast
Cherish you till the end of time

(Chorus)

I favorite You In my soul
————————————

I am losing my mind
Over your love
I tried your number
Three too many times

You know me
Very good
I love you
For you

(Chorus)
This is my promise
I favorite you in my soul
I sleep with you at night
Wishing you are with me

Something is beautiful
When you call my name
When you read my mind
When you reach out to me
Oh how I need you

And I look at your picture
You gave me one summer night
Flowing my mind beautiful sunrise

(Chorus)

In my Soul
————————

I give my life
To the extraordinary time
that this river just
keeps on knocking
At my heart

I live I love
I hold you in my arms
I think about us
How your love amazes me

(Chorus)
'Cause In My Soul
You are my only song
Playing destiny

Just take my hand
Let's dance the night away
Let's be us tonight
Close that world news
Outside that door

Every day you are my beautiful
Every day you are my incredible
My harmony glazed through those
Sky lines

(Chorus)

You Are My Easy Light
———————————-

Something beautiful
Something ordinary
One life one love
You and I are dreaming
About tomorrow

We built a bridge
Of our love tonight
To last on forever
Beautiful as ever

(Chorus)
You are my easy light
Shining me brighter
Warming my heart
Lifting me up when I am
Down under those waters
Just floating around

This place of us
This saving me
I want to rock with you
All day long

Baby I need you too
I love you too
You are my destiny
And My promise
I promise you this

(Chorus)

Write you a song
————————

What brings me to you
What holds me up
Singing me back to you
Baby you are all I ever need

Just to see you smile
Just to hold you closer
Just to feel your sweet touch
On my heart

(Chorus)
And here I am
Sitting on this bed
Laying close to you
Looking at your beautiful
Eyes and all I ever want to do
Is write you a song
To sing it to you

You are my everything
The garden of love
The light through my soul
The river through my mind

Best friend for life
My endless hope
Amazing grace
Tender and Sweet

(Chorus)

Crystal bowl
―――――-

Crying into the night
Beating my heart into something
You gave up on us many years ago
I seen many roads

I have tried to forget you
But my mind keeps on going
On you baby line by line
Till my heart stops beating

(Chorus)
So I ask that crystal bowl
I found in that circus tent
Our family our future
Our love and all we give

When forever is over
I will know then
For now I still love you
Getting myself into you again

Holding on to what have been
To what we have
You and I so much beautiful
Love that last

(Chorus)

Temptation
—————

Looking so beautiful
Like an angel through the night
Saving amazing grace
Something without a doubt

Every chance you get
Every song you light up
It comes so naturally
Flowing free

(Chorus)
In this ten foot tall
Wings flying through
Those seas
Temptation is your key

You take me places
I never been before
You hold me right
When the weather
Gets too dark in town

Thanks to you I am alive
Loving you Is so much more
Loving you is all you are to me
You are my home

(Chorus)
In this ten foot tall
Wings flying through
Those seas
Temptation is your key

Sunshine and glamour
————————————-

The clouds are rolling
We twist and turn
Rolling with the motion
Under the moonlight

(Chorus)
Baby you are
Sunshine and glamour
Tonight and always
You are to me

I give my heart to ♥ you
One beat at the time
One day over the summer
You are my rock

One perfect day
One morning afternoon
Anytime anywhere
Anything if you want me too
I will be right there for you

(Chorus)

Baby Save Me
——————-

(Chorus)
Baby save me
One day at saints time
You are my beautiful grace
You add best ingredients
In my life

You are my true saint
My saving grace
And I am blue as I can get
But when you come by
My heart you bring me to life

I crave for you
Need you too
You are my song
My bright light
My easiness in my soul

(Chorus)
(Repeat Chorus 2-3 more times
And first line of the chorus)

Give me five million reasons
———————————————

(Chorus)
Give me five million reasons
Why not to let you go
Just a strong emotion
Beating so hard
Like a drum

Every wave
Every tornado
Looking so much stronger
Our love is just another
Passage In time

Proven by ten story lines
In that written book
Destiny is our life
Love that fills those serenity's
And I love you so

(Chorus)
(Repeat Chorus 2-3 Times plus
First line of the chorus)

Epitome
———-

Distance of my memory
Life with you is so sweet
Good night afternoons
By that fireplace
Laying on that couch
Holding on forever

You talk to me
Loving me
Breathing me in
And I am breathing you in

(Chorus)
Honey, love you
With all my heart
Taken by your smile
Each day at the time
You are my epitome

And I love you so
Want to hold you so close
Till day break
If that makes perfect sense

I need you I miss you I want you
My heart keeps on Beating for you
Every time you are Closer to me

(Chorus)

www.ingramcontent.com/pod-product-compliance
Lightning Source LLC
Chambersburg PA
JSW060503110426
/38CB00055B/2607